WILLOW PROJECTS
FOR BEGINNERS

Wendy Thorner

MID WALES Willow

I'll take this opportunity to embarrass my husband, Graham, who not only cheered me on from the start but who has also had to endure my frequent arguments with the laptop; our son, Ben, who patiently introduced me to the tortuous intricacies of Microsoft Office, and then came up with some great ideas in putting this book together; our daughter, Chloe, who helped with the business in the early days, giving me time to work on this book in its embryonic stage; and our dear friend, Fran, who encouraged me to make basket making my career choice in the first place.

Thank you!

ISBN:9798805080167

CONTENTS

Introduction and how to use this book ·· 1

Willow, where to buy and soaking times ··· 2

Before you begin ·· 6

Tools··· 7

BASKET PROJECTS

Table basket ·· 9

Wastepaper basket ··· 11

Apple basket ··· 13

Shopping basket ·· 15

Log basket ··· 17

Oval shopping basket ·· 20

Oval gathering basket ··· 26

'Square' shopping basket ··· 28

Simplified frame basket ·· 43

FUN PROJECTS

Dragonfly ··· 50

Hearts 1 and 2 ·· 56

Bunting ··· 59

Christmas··· 63

Kissing bough ··· 64

Wreath··· 67

Star ··· 69

Wands ··· 71

Christmas tree ··· 72

Getting started (the base) ·· 75

Staking up and the upsett ·· 79

Siding·· 84

Borders ·· 89

Handles ··· 97

Recommended reading ··· 105

Also by the author

To see what Wendy is currently working on, visit her facebook and Instagram pages:

www.facebook.com/midwaleswillow

wendythorner.basketmaker

and her website:

www.midwaleswillow.co.uk

INTRODUCTION

I've always loved weaving, from corn to cane to rushes, but from the time I planted those very first cuttings and got my first crop of willow (pictured above), my love affair with willow grew. Virtually everything I know I've learned from books and by experience. I started my willow business—Mid Wales Willow— in 2009, but before then I had already come up with the idea of producing basket making kits. These kits have proved a huge success, and the reason why I have compiled this book: most of the 'kits' are in here, plus other projects, with all the step by step instructions that have made them so popular.

HOW TO USE THIS BOOK

I have kept the instructions as simple as possible, and rely heavily on photographs to teach you the processes, using coloured willow rods to make things clearer. There are some very good books on willow work that will take you forward (see page 105), and basket making courses as well, but I am concerned only with getting you started and learning the basics. To this end I've avoided as far as possible using unnecessary terminology, so you won't find a glossary!

Each project is presented as a recipe and, like any good recipe book, I don't repeat the same steps again and again, but direct you to the appropriate pages, the sides of which have a coloured bar so as to make finding them that bit easier. You can start with any of the 'round' baskets, though I have ordered them in terms of difficulty. Or go straight for the 'fun' projects, which are all easy and also very useful for using up any leftover brown willow from a basket project.

You will notice the red circles ● that come with most recipes: these are there to give you a rough idea of the size of the willow you need— height alone isn't much of a guide as thicknesses vary within a bolt of willow, and more noticeably from supplier to supplier. In basket making generally, the weavers should be thinner than the uprights, but not necessarily much thinner.

Now all you have to do is buy the willow— but first read pages 2-7, and especially page 6.

WILLOW

Willow is sold in 'bolts', but smaller amounts can be purchased. A rough guide is given by the supplier as to the quantity of rods per bolt. For the purposes of this book you may need to purchase some of the following:

BUFF WILLOW

This is willow that has been boiled and the bark removed. I would strongly advise that beginners use this, as it requires very little soaking and grips well when woven. The most useful sizes for the purposes of this book are '4ft' and '5ft'. The sizes refer to the height of the willow after grading. A '4ft' bundle will have rods that are 3ft-4ft in height. They will be of different thicknesses, and sometimes forked, but all are useful. Generally speaking, the taller the bundle, the thicker the rods. Some 5ft rods are very thin, so you will see why in most of the recipes I recommend 4ft/5ft, as thicknesses can be the same.

BROWN WILLOW

'Brown' refers to the natural willow that has been dried. If it is fresh cut it will be called 'green', but it is unsuitable for baskets in this state, as it will shrink as it dries and the basket will be loose. The brown you are most likely to be offered— and the best for these projects—is Black Maul (pictured right). You will need mainly 3ft brown, but 4ft for some of the projects—see the list of ingredients for what you would like to make.

WILLOW

STEAMED WILLOW (far left) is willow that has been steamed, so it still retains the bark but is now a dark chocolate colour.

WHITE WILLOW (left) has had the bark removed.

OTHER BROWN WILLOW

Pictured right are some green varieties which can be bought from some growers: Brittany Green, Dicky Meadows and Flanders Red. They add variety and are generally thinner than Black Maul.

WHERE TO BUY

Coates Willow www.english**willow**baskets.co.uk

Musgrove Willows www.**musgrovewillows**.co.uk

Somerset Willow www.**willowgrowers**.co.uk

Also on offer in the spring is 'green' willow (fresh cut) and 'semi– dried'. The latter, depending on how dry it is, may not need soaking at all and be ready for weaving; we call this stage 'clung': that is, the willow has reached the point where it will not shrink in size but be perfect for weaving, in that it doesn't snap, retains its colour and doesn't shrink when dried. (Soaking dried willow will always cause some colour loss.) I make all my baskets with our own willow and mostly in the spring, when the willow is still 'clung'.

TIP After the main growers have cut the willow they have to sort it, which takes an inordinate amount of time. If you visit an online site, and it says 'Out of Stock', it doesn't necessarily mean there isn't any, just that they haven't sorted enough to keep up with demand. Musgrove have a useful tool on these occasions, whereby you can click 'Notify Me', and you will automatically receive an email when the willow is available. Or just phone them!

SOAKING THE WILLOW

You will need somewhere to soak the willow. If you're only using small amounts, then a soaking bag is O.K. (Available from some willow suppliers.)

I use a galvanised water trough which is fed from a water butt overflow, but an old bath should be adequate. Failing that, a child's paddling pool is perfectly fine, or get some heavy duty polythene (builders' or the type used for encasing silage) or pond liner, and prop the edges up with some blocks. Whatever you use, the willow must be submerged. Plastic crates, weighted with stones, are ideal for holding the willow down.

After **soaking**—the willow will still seem stiff—all the willow should be wrapped in a damp cloth or polythene to **mellow** overnight, though 4 or 5 hours for buff and white should be enough.

SOAKING TIMES

(Recipe ingredients are fairly accurate, but you might like to soak a little more of the buff or white as unused rods can be dried and used again.)

BUFF AND WHITE WILLOW

Generally, **1.5 hours** is about right for **4ft**.

And **2 hours** is about right for **5-6ft**.

Don't oversoak as the willow may deteriorate.

STEAMED WILLOW

3ft will need about **36 hours**.

4ft will need about **2 days**.

Steamed willow is tricky in that it is prone to shred the bark if oversoaked. Times given are for mild weather, so keep an eye if very warm and maybe soak a little less.

BROWN WILLOW (BLACK MAUL)

3ft will need about **2 days**.

4ft will need about **3 days**.

Some suppliers advocate 1 day per foot, but the above times have always worked, no matter what the weather.

OTHER BROWN WILLOW

A day a foot for **Brittany Green** and **Dicky Meadows**, but **Flanders Red** may well need about **2 days a foot**, though less in warm weather.

A test for readiness is to kink up the tip— if it cracks, leave it longer. However, individual rods will misbehave no matter how long you soak them, so trial and error have always worked for me.

REMEMBER TO LEAVE ALL WILLOW TO MELLOW, AS ADVISED ON PAGE 4.

BEFORE YOU BEGIN

Here's the not so interesting—but necessary—stuff you need to know.

BUFF WILLOW is a wonderful material for beginners, and is widely used by expert basket makers. HOWEVER, **it does dry out really quickly**, so avoid working in a warm place, and keep a damp cloth handy for wiping the uprights every so often. If you have to leave your work for a while, wrap tightly in a damp cloth or polythene. Before commencing the border I would soak the whole basket for at least 30 minutes, otherwise you may find that the uprights have dried out and snap when bent. On the plus side, any buff rods you don't use can be dried out and used again, so always soak more.

WHITE WILLOW must be treated in the same way as **buff**.

BROWN WILLOW is what is generally used, along with buff, for making baskets. It doesn't dry out quickly so there's no need for dampening or re-soaking. On the negative side, it cannot be dried out and re-soaked successfully for future projects. However, any surplus could be used in making some of the fun projects on pages 50 to 74.

GREEN WILLOW cannot be used in baskets as it will shrink too much but, as it keeps its colour when dried, use it for some of the projects on pages 50 to 74.

STEAMED WILLOW, like brown, is not so prone to drying out, but any surplus cannot be dried as it cannot be re-soaked, so pages 50 to 74 again for any surplus.

HEDGEROW MATERIAL is a wonderful resource for colour and texture, and something I used to use a lot of in my own baskets. Farmers are discouraged from cutting their hedges until September, so there is an abundance of material in late August: willow, hazel, birch and ash, to name but a few, all waiting to be gathered and stripped of leaves by you. Normally you wouldn't cut until November, but in the case of hedgerows that would be too late—the farmer would have got there before you! Now be patient and let the material dry a little. With willow, when the rods are showing signs of wrinkle, we call this stage '**clung**'. The material is now perfect for use and shouldn't shrink anymore. With hedgerow material that stage isn't always obvious, but it's great in its 'green' stage for kissing boughs (page 64) and wreaths (page 67) if you're unsure about using it in a basket.

(Remember to ask the landowner's permission before helping yourself.)

Finally, when looking at the ingredients for each project, the '**butt**' refers to the fat end of the willow rod. (The '**tip**' is the thin end.)

TOOLS

You can get by without any specific tools for basket making, though it's handy to have them if you're planning on doing a lot of work. Named below are the tools I use regularly—and all you will need for the purposes of this book—and written in brackets are alternatives you probably already have.

Bodkin (knitting needle, screwdriver, bradawl)

You will need this for making gaps in the work; especially useful when doing a basket border or inserting uprights into the base.

Angled snips (secateurs, old scissors)

I use these for cutting the willow to size and trimming.

Rapping iron (small hammer)

Necessary for compressing the weave to prevent gaps.

Weight (large pebble, rock, brick, tin of beans/dog food)

You will need a weight to hold the basket steady as you work.

Plus you will also need a **ruler/tape measure**, and some **elastic** to tie the tops of the uprights of the basket as you work—2.5cm wide is perfect, but a chain of elastic bands will do. Something like a block about 1cm high for beginning a border will be needed for baskets. **Petroleum jelly** is also useful. You will, of course, take all necessary precautions when using tools. However, if you work at a table—like me—be very careful placing your tools: my feet have had several near misses with bodkins, rappers, snips and weights.

(Square work only) Screw block

There isn't really a good alternative for this, but you won't be doing any square work until you have mastered round and oval baskets, so you'll have plenty of time to get one made.

Below is mine made out of the offcuts of 2 oak beams. I really ought to ditch it as the sides aren't straight and don't grip the base sticks uniformly, but we've been working together for such a long time that I don't know if I can bear to part with it. (Besides, it has all the marks I've made for positioning base sticks for favourite baskets.)

To make your own screw block you'll need:

2 x 2ft (60cms) lengths of 3x2 inch timber (preferably planed)—a good builders' merchant will cut them to size.

2 x bolts, at least 5 inches (12.5cms) long, and 2 wing nuts to fit.

To construct, lay the timbers on top of each other, measure 2 inches in from ends, and 1.5 inches in from edge, and draw a cross. Drill both holes with an appropriate size drill bit, until you reach and mark the next block. Then remove the top block and drill through the second. Use the bolts to connect and the wing nuts to tighten.

TABLE BASKET

Dimensions: D.35cm x H.15 cm

INGREDIENTS

24 x 4ft/5ft buff for uprights, the butts of which should just sit inside this circle.

About 40 x 4ft thin/medium buff rods for weaving the base and waling, a few of which very thin for starting the base.

6 x 20cm buff sticks for the base, the butts of which should just sit inside this circle.

100gms 3ft Black Maul.

IMPORTANT Soak willow as advised on pages 4&5 and read page 6.

TABLE BASKET

1. **Page 75** ⬜ for instructions on how to complete the **base**.

2. **Page 79** ▬ and follow the instructions for **staking up**. (Slype 24 uprights on the '**back**'.)

3. Now **page 80** ▬ for the first round of **waling**.

4. **Page 84** ▬ and follow the instructions for **slewing**. Concentrate on keeping the uprights flowing outwards, not inwards.

5. **Page 80** ▬ again for another round of **waling**—use the slightly thicker weavers to control the uprights.

6. **Page 89** ▬ for a **3 rod border** or, if you're confident enough, **page 93** ▬ for a **5 rod behind 1 border**. Make sure you soak your basket for at least half an hour before attempting the border if you think the uprights might have dried out.

7. Trim ends so that they lie, as far as possible, against an upright.

WASTEPAPER BASKET

Dimensions: Ht. 30cm x D. 28cm

INGREDIENTS

24 x 4ft / 5ft buff for uprights, the butts of which should just sit inside this circle.

About 40 x 4ft thin/medium buff rods for weaving the base and waling, a few of which very thin for starting the base.

6 x 20cm buff sticks for the base, the butts of which should just sit inside this circle.

350gms 3ft Black Maul or 3ft steamed willow. (Basket pictured is made with steamed, but instructions show Black Maul.)

IMPORTANT Soak willow as advised on pages 4&5 and read page 6.

WASTEPAPER BASKET

1. **Page 75** [   ] for instructions on how to complete the **base**.

2. **Page 79** [   ] and follow the instructions for **staking up**. (Slype 24 uprights on the '**belly**'.)

3. Now **page 80** [   ] for the first round of **waling**.

4. **Page 84** [   ] and follow the instructions for **slewing**. Concentrate on keeping the uprights flowing slightly outwards, not inwards.

5. **Page 80** [   ] again for another round of **waling**—use the slightly thicker weavers to control the uprights.

6. **Page 89** [   ] for a **3 rod border** or, if you're confident enough, **page 93** [   ] for a **5 rod behind 1 border**. Make sure you soak your basket for at least half an hour before attempting the border if you think the uprights might have dried out.

7. Trim ends so that they lie, as far as possible, against an upright.

APPLE BASKET

Dimensions: H.38cm D.32cm

INGREDIENTS

24 x 4ft/5ft buff for uprights, the butts of which should just sit inside this circle.

6 long 4ft/5ft buff rods for handles, the butts of which should cover this circle.

About 60 x 4ft/5ft thin/medium buff rods for weaving the base and waling, a few of which very thin for starting the base.

6 x 30cm buff sticks for the base, the butts of which should just sit inside this circle.

350gms 3ft Black Maul or 3ft steamed willow.

IMPORTANT Soak willow as advised on pages 4&5 and read page 6.

APPLE BASKET

1. **Page 75**  for instructions on how to complete the **base**.

2. **Page 79** and follow the instructions for **staking up**.
(Slype 24 uprights on the '**belly**'.)

3. **Page 80** for the first round of **waling**. Repeat—12 rods in total.

You might like to try the more professional method on **page 82** .

4. Now **page 84** and follow the instructions for **slewing**. Concentrate on keeping the uprights vertical.

5. **Page 80** again for another round of **waling**, using the slightly thicker weavers to control the uprights. Repeat—12 rods in total.

6. **Page 89** for a **3 rod border** or, if you're confident enough, **page 93** for a **5 rod behind 1** border. Make sure you soak your basket for at least half an hour before attempting the border if you think the uprights might have dried out.

7. Trim ends so that they lie, as far as possible, against an upright.

8. Go to **'Handles for Log Baskets'** on **page 102** .

SHOPPING BASKET

Dimensions: 38cm x 38cm

INGREDIENTS

24 x 4ft/5ft buff uprights, the butts of which should just sit inside this circle.

About 100 x 4ft thin/medium buff rods for weaving the base, siding and waling, a few of which very thin for starting the base. Put 24 of the tallest, thickest of these to one side for the **French Randing** weave.

6 x 20cm buff sticks for the base, the butts of which should just cover this circle.

8 long, medium 5ft buff for wrapping the handle.

Buff handle 80-85cm long, the butt of which should cover this circle.

2 x 30cm sticks for handle liners—anything will do—to create spaces for the handle to go. The butts should cover this circle.

IMPORTANT Soak willow as advised on pages 4&5 and read page 6.

SHOPPING BASKET

1. **Page 75**  for instructions on how to complete the **base**.

2. **Page 79** 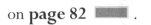 and follow the instructions for **staking up**. (Slype 24 uprights on the '**back**'.)

3. **Page 80** for the first round of **3 rod wale**. You might like to try the more professional method on **page 82** .

4. **Page 84** and follow the instructions for **slewing**. Keep the uprights flowing outwards initially, but start to encourage them to be more vertical later, else the basket will be too wide. Stop at about 13cm height.

5. **Page 80** for another round of **waling**.

6. Insert the (slyped) handle liners beside, and to the left of, an upright and opposite each other. You will need to ease the handle liners up as you work, otherwise you'll have difficulty removing them later: try greasing them with petroleum jelly. You will now treat the upright and the liner as one when you weave.

7. **Page 86** and follow the instructions for **French Randing**. Keep the uprights vertical at this stage.

8 Another round of **waling**—**page 80** .

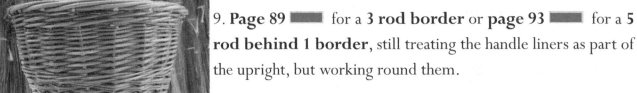

9. **Page 89** for a **3 rod border** or **page 93** for a **5 rod behind 1 border**, still treating the handle liners as part of the upright, but working round them.

10. Remove the handle liners, trim and then go to **page 97** and follow the instructions for **Handle/Shopper**.

LOG BASKET

Dimensions: H.45cm x D.42cm

INGREDIENTS

24 x 5ft buff uprights, the butts of which should just sit inside this circle.

6 x 35cm buff sticks for the base, the butts of which should cover this circle.

50x 4ft/5ft tall buff rods for waling, the butts of which should fit inside this circle.

50x 4ft/5ft buff rods for weaving the base, some thin and long.

400gms of 4ft Black Maul for slewing.

24 tall 5ft rods in steamed, white or any natural willow such as 5ft Dicky Meadows and Flanders Red (as used in this basket), the butts of which should fit inside this circle.

24 as above, but different to your first choice.

Length of wood or any object that is approximately 60cm long and 4-6cm wide, to act as a 'mould' for the handle gaps.

IMPORTANT Soak willow as advised on pages 4&5 and read page 6.

LOG BASKET

1. **Page 75** ▭ for instructions on how to complete the **base**.

2. **Page 79** ▬ and follow the instructions for staking up. (Slype 24 uprights on the '**belly**'.)

3. Now **page 80** ▬ for the first round of **waling.**

 Repeat—12 buff rods in total. You might like to try the more professional method on **page 82** ▬ .

4. **Page 84** ▬ and follow the instructions for **slewing**, using the 400gms of Black Maul. Concentrate on keeping the uprights vertical.

5. **Page 80** ▬ and use 12 more buff rods for a **3 rod wale**.

6. You will now need the 2 bundles of 24 rods to complete 2 rounds of **French Randing**—see **page 86** ▬ . To achieve the chequered effect, take 12 of each colour and add them alternately—as I have in the instructions. When you have completed the first layer, repeat, but with the opposite colour this time— green in this picture, but it would be purple for a chequered effect. You could, of course, use 4 colours, 12 of each, if you wish.

7. After the second round you will have something like this. Remember to check the height to ensure it's even.

8. **Page 80** ▬ for a **3 rod wale** using 12 buff rods.

9. Lay the piece of wood across the middle of the basket as shown, choosing a 'clean' gap: that is not near where you finished waling. Select 12 rods for a 3 rod wale and put the tips together. Now cut them 80cm long, removing the butts. Select 8 of the longest of these butts, slype the thin end and insert one to the left of each upright either side of the wood as shown (4 each side). This is to strengthen the handle gap. Repeat for the opposite side. (You will have to find 4 more butt ends of similar thickness—they don't have to be soaked.)

10. Take 3 rods and start the wale—tip first—from the first upright AFTER a reinforced handle gap. Start 3 more on the opposite side. Go over the top of the wood with each set as shown, waling round the uprights and butt sticks as one.

11. STOP waling at this point ★ (or earlier if the rods run out) before you reach the second handle space: joining in butts on top of the handle looks very messy, so trim and join in before climbing over the handle with each set of rods.

15. Rap down very gently—the wood stays in until the border is completed—and trim the 16 handle strengthening sticks close to the waling as shown. You can use your rapper to tap them level with the wale.

16. **Page 93** ▬▬ for a **5 rod behind 1 border**.

OVAL SHOPPER

(I wouldn't attempt oval work until you have completed at least 2 round baskets.)

Dimensions to handle: 38cm x 30cm x H.34cm

INGREDIENTS

28 x 4ft/5ft buff uprights, the butts of which should just sit inside this circle.

8 long, medium 4ft/5ft buff for handle wrapping.

About 60 x 4ft buff rods for weaving the base and waling, a few very thin for starting the base.

7 x 23cm buff sticks for the base, the butts of which should just sit inside this circle.

3 x 37cm buff sticks for the base, the butts of which should just sit inside this circle.

350gms 3ft Black Maul.

Buff handle 80-85cm long, the butt of which should cover this circle.

2 x 30cm sticks for handle liners—anything will do—to create spaces for the handle to go. The butts should cover this circle.

IMPORTANT Soak willow as advised on pages 4&5 and read page 6.

OVAL SHOPPER

1. Take the 7 shorter sticks and using a bodkin, pierce the middle of all of them. Thread the longer 3 through the holes in these 7 so that AC=BC, and the shorter sticks are arranged like so.

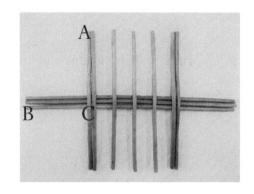

2. Now take 2 of the longest, thinnest buff weavers and insert the tips (the thin ends) in through the gap beside the 3 longer sticks.

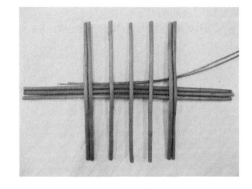

3. Take the right-hand rod over 3 sticks and the left-hand rod under.

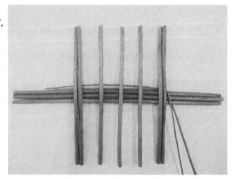

4. Take the right-hand rod over the left hand-rod and 2 sticks, and the left hand rod under 2 sticks. Continue pairing as usual. (**Page 75** ⬜ .)

5. When the rods 'run out', you have to join in two more. Do this at the same time, and always on the straight edge of the base.

6. Continue pairing in this way until you've been round twice.

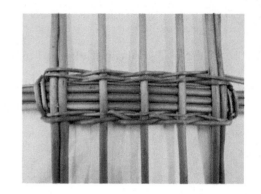

7. Now start dividing the sticks.

8. Continue pairing in this way until the sticks are evenly spaced. Concentrate on crowning the base slightly. Use 8 rods in total, always starting and finishing on the straight side.

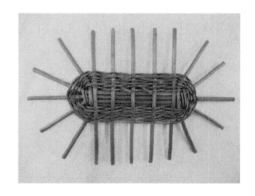

9. You may notice as you work that the base has developed a bit of a twist. To counteract this we're now going to 'reverse pair': essentially it's like twisting string in the opposite direction, so instead of pulling to the front, you now pull to the back, still working clockwise. Insert 2 new tips but this time pull to the back rather than the front. Start 2 new rods on the other straight side and chase each pair round. (8 rods in total.)

10. Normal pairing again, starting 2 pairs on each straight side. Continue alternating pairing to reverse pairing every 8 rods.

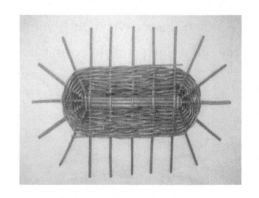

11. You may not always be able to join in two sets of rods when you near the edge of the base– gauge the remaining space and maybe start only one pair if there's little room left. Stop when the weaving is almost at the edge.

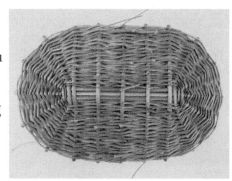

12. Trim the sticks and the weaving.

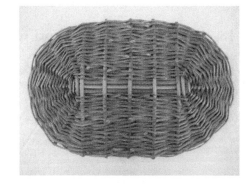

13. Slype the 28 uprights on the '**belly**'.

14. Insert each rod slype side down like so, with one rod either side of the centre stick, but otherwise only one to the side of each stick on the straight sides.

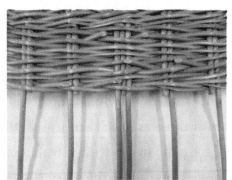

15. Insert the remaining uprights on the curve as shown.

16. Prick up the straight sides first and tie.

17. Now prick up the end rods and tie them as high as possible.

18. **Page 80** ▭ for a **3 rod wale**.

Better still turn to **page 82** ▭ and do the more professional wale.

19. Before you begin waling please note that the two pairs of central uprights count as one, so don't weave into the gap between them. Use 12 rods in total.

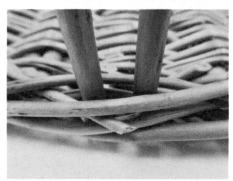

20. Insert the greased handle liners in the space between the central uprights each side—now you can see why they've been treated as one: this is where the handle will finally go. You will continue to treat them as one when you do the next weave. It's an idea to grease the handle liners with petroleum jelly, and move them up as you weave, otherwise they could get stuck.

21. **Page 84** ▭ and follow the instructions for **slewing**. Try to ensure the uprights are evenly spaced. The height is up to you, but I stopped slewing when the basket reached 16cm high after rapping down. Check level.

22. **Page 82** ▬ for the final **wale**. You will need 12 thicker weavers for this. Rap down, and measure the height carefully.

23. Cut the upright to the left of each handle liner down to the waling.

24. **Page 93** ▬ and follow the instructions for **5 rod behind 1 border**.

(You need to treat the handle liner as part of the upright when you reach it, though the handle liner remains where it is.)

25. Remove the handle liners— they have served their purpose and you should now have 2 clear spaces into which you are going to insert the handle.

26. **Page 97** ▬ and follow the instructions for **Handle/ Shopper** to finish the basket.

OVAL GATHERING BASKET

Dimensions to handle: 47cm x 30cm x H.30cm

INGREDIENTS:

As for oval shopper (page 20), except for:

32 (not 28) x 4ft/5ft buff uprights, the butts of which should just sit inside this circle. ●

100gms (not 350gms) 3ft Black Maul.

1. Turn to page 20 and follow instructions 1– 14.

2. Insert the remaining uprights either side a base stick on the curve as shown.

3. Now page 24, instructions 16-19.

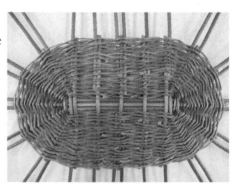

OVAL GATHERING BASKET

4. Now you need to shape the ends of the basket. All the uprights forming the curve need to be gently eased out but still left tied. Take your time with this until you get the shape you'd like—the further you pull them out, the more defined will be the drop from the handle to the ends.

5. **Page 84**  and follow the instructions for **slewing**. You will notice as you work that the ends are lower than the sides—the uprights are lower, so this is inevitable and perfect for this design. (If you want a level top, introduce an extra rod as you start the curve, and drop the bottom rod when you reach the straight side again.)

6. **Page 82** for final **waling**. You will need 12 thicker weavers for this. Rap down, and measure the height carefully: opposite sides— and ends—must be equal.

7. Cut the upright to the left of each handle liner down to the waling.

Page 93 and follow the instructions for **5 rod behind 1 border**. You need to treat the handle liner as part of the upright when you reach it, though the handle liner remains where it is.

Remove the handle liners— they have served their purpose and you should now have 2 clear spaces into which you are going to insert the handle.

Page 97 and follow the instructions for **Handle/Shopper** to finish the basket.

SQUARE SHOPPER

Dimensions: 30cm x 35cm x H.32cm

I wasn't going to include 'square' basketry (the term refers to the corners, not the shape) in this book for two reasons:

Firstly, they're a lot trickier than 'round' baskets and secondly you require a block in order to make one (see page 8). That being said, I have included a method that was taught to me by Pippa Scott, who had learned it from Mary Butcher, and it is by far the easiest way of doing square work. However, it does require an awful lot of space either side of you in which to work—about 4ft.

I wouldn't attempt square work until you have completed several round baskets and different borders.

SQUARE SHOPPER

INGREDIENTS

8 x buff base sticks, 45cm long. The butts should cover this circle. **(Do not soak.)**

18 x 4ft/5ft buff rods for uprights, the butts of which should **just cover** this circle.

16 x 4ft/5ft buff rods for uprights, the butts of which should **sit inside** this circle.

24 x 4ft/5ft buff rods for the base, at least 110cm long and the butts should fit in this circle.

2 x 4ft/5ft thin, long buff rods.

24 x 4ft/5ft rods for the wale, the butts of which should fit inside this circle.

Handle, 80–85cm long, the butt of which should cover this circle.

8 x 4ft/5ft medium buff rods for wrapping the handle.

Handle liners.

250 gm 3ft brown Black Maul.

As I have already said on page 5, you should always soak a little more than the amounts given. This is especially true with the buff used in square work.

IMPORTANT Soak willow as advised on pages 4&5 (and read page 6), but not the base sticks as they have to be strong, so keep them dry. Very gently ease them until they are as straight as you can make them—don't worry too much if they go in and out a bit.

THE BASE

1. Take 4 of the base sticks with the thickest butts and lay them with the tips facing you alternately with the butts of the thinnest sticks.

2. Slype the butts of the thinner sticks and arrange as shown, with the tips of the thicker sticks.

3. First tighten the screws on your block so that the sticks do not drop to the bottom when inserted.

Insert the first stick into your block and tighten that end.

4. Insert the second stick 3.5cm along from that.

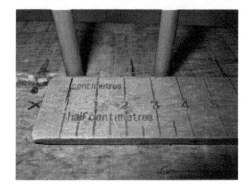

5. Continue in this manner, inserting sticks every 3.5cms, until all 8 are in, butts and tips alternating. (The last stick should have been placed at 24.5cms.) Use your rapper to tap the wing nuts round to hold the sticks as tightly as possible. Now tap the top of the sticks to make sure they are in as tight as they will go.

6. It is essential when weaving the base that you measure the width of the base frequently. Before you begin, measure the width at the bottom of the sticks, and then move the ruler up high, and adjust accordingly. Always measure at least 20cms above the weave to get an accurate picture.

7. Take a long, thin buff rod, and insert it tip first through the first gap, so that about half is left.

8. Now bring the tip round to the front, as shown.

9. Take the tip behind the second stick and back to the front.

10. Take the butt behind the third stick and back to the front. Continue pairing…

11. …until you reach the end.

12. Now take the tip to the back…

13. …and wrap it round the last stick and out to the back again.

14. Wrap the butt round the last stick (over the tip) and back to the front again.

15. Take the butt to the back and leave.

16. You will now need the bundle of 18 uprights. Select one and insert the butt as shown.

17. This part is very important, and must be repeated with every upright you insert. From the above picture you can see that the upright has been woven into the base. However, this must be done with great care. You mustn't kink the upright, nor must you allow the sticks to move. Hold the third stick as you ease the upright to the back, and then the fourth stick as you ease it to the front. Continue in this way to the end and leave it. 18. Now insert the butt end of the second upright on top of the first, but this time against the eighth stick, and pointing in the opposite direction. Weave as before.

19. You will now have 2 uprights, pointing in opposite directions—and can see why you need so much space to work! Rap down.

20. You will now need the 24 buff rods for the base. Insert the butt of one 3 sticks in as shown.

21. Weave in and out and when you get to the last stick, hold the stick firmly as you pull the rod round tightly. Continue to weave in and out, remembering to hold each stick in position as you do so.

22. Finish at the back, but never against an end stick.

23. Insert the butt of another rod 3 sticks in from the right, and weave in and out again, going left first, until this rod runs out.

24. Finish at the back.

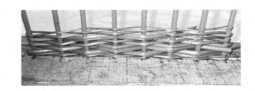

25. Insert the butt of a third rod 2 sticks in from the left. Now weave as before…

26. …and finish at the back. Rap down.

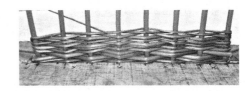

27. Insert an upright and weave as before, controlling the sticks, and letting go at the end. (I always get an overwhelming temptation to weave it round—and sometimes do—so don't!)

28. Insert another upright from the left and weave as before.

29. Rap down.

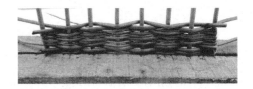

30. Now insert a rod, butt first, by the stick second from the right, and weave to the left and so on as before.

31. And third from the left…

32. …then third from the right.

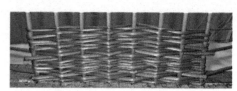

33. Rap down, particularly in the middle.

Now insert more uprights as before, and rods as before—if you look at the back you can see a pattern is emerging, so continue that pattern for inserting rods.

34. Apart from checking the width of the sticks frequently, as explained on page 30, you should also turn the block now and then and look along it: are the sticks in a straight line? If not, gently ease them as necessary. Try to keep the gaps between them roughly equal.

35. If the rod splits when taking it around an end stick, discard and replace with one of the spares you wisely prepared.

36. When you have inserted your last pair of uprights—18 altogether—you will have something like this. Rap down/ease up until the height is the same all the way along.

37. Take the other thin rod and, just as you did at the start, insert the tip half way through to the right of the first stick and wrap it round and pair with the butt end.

38. Stop when you get this far, with the butt against the end stick.

39. Take the tip to the back, wrap round the end stick, then behind, in front, behind and leave.

40. Now take the butt behind and back to the front. Now slype the end and kink…

41. …and insert like so. Rap down and check height.

42. Now you will need the other 16 uprights. Slype them all on the belly. Trim all the base sticks back to the weave and insert 8 of the rods as shown, using petroleum jelly and a bodkin to help you. You will realise that there is only room for 7 rods, but select the base sticks with the widest gap between them and insert another there.

43. You will now have 8 uprights as evenly spaced as possible. (Remember, most of these photos are cropped—don't go cutting the uprights! If I included the whole picture you wouldn't see the detail.)

44. Prick each upright with your bodkin, slightly above the stick, and pull forward and release.

45. Trim the butt ends of the woven uprights as shown.

46. Take each of the woven uprights in turn, pull to the front, and release.

47. Release the base from the block, and trim the sticks to the weave. Now insert the last 8 uprights as previously described.

48. Now it's time to gather up the uprights. Ideally use 3 lengths of elastic. Leaving the 8 that form each corner, first gather up both long sides and tie, and then both short sides and tie further up. Finally gather all corners and tie together further up. Now trim the base.

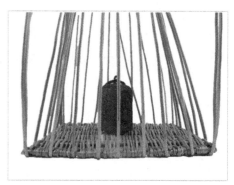

49. Ease the 8 corner uprights vertical, but keep them tied in. If your base isn't sitting flat, place it on the floor and ease your foot in to step on it—that usually does the trick. If not, hold against the edge of a table and bend it until you get it the way you want.

50. Take 12 of the rods set aside for the wale. Insert 3 tips either side as shown and start waling, making sure to keep the uprights vertical. Join in and finish on the long side. Rap down and measure Ease up as necessary. Insert the greased handle liners to the left of the 5th upright on both long sides.

51. Now you need the 3ft bundle of Black Maul for slewing: **page 84** ▭ . Before commencing, please read these instructions as the process is slightly different for square baskets. Insert a butt of a long rod as shown.

52. When you get to the corner, hold the 2 corner rods upright with your left hand as you weave with your right.

53. At this point on the short side, join in the second rod.

54. Weave round the next corner with both rods. Then drop them and start a new rod and join in as before.

55. There is a tendency for corners to build up higher than the sides, so a good way to offset this is not to join in just before a corner...

56. ...but wait until you go round it.

57. Now it's all about shaping. Measure both diameters and ensure they're the same. If not, measure the sides and adjust appropriately. Keep the sides tied in, but release the corners when you think they're held in position. There is a tendency for the sides to want to flop out, so keeping them tied in helps you in weaving them upright. Meanwhile, the corners want to go in, so remember to use your hand to keep them upright.

58. When you have reached the desired height, (remember waling and the border will add an extra 3-4cms) finish slewing and adjust for height.

59. Now do another 3 rod wale (12 rods in total) and adjust for height.

4 ROD BEHIND 2 BORDER FOR SQUARE BASKETS

60. First use your small block to bend down and raise all the uprights as you have on previous baskets.

Take the second upright along on the long side, and bend it down behind 2 uprights.

61. Now repeat with the next 3 uprights—leave the handle liner in place as shown.

62. We will continue with coloured rods to make the process clearer.

63. Take the pink rod in front of 2 uprights and behind 1.

64. Lay the yellow down beside it.

65. Now do the same with the blue rod and lay the red down beside it.

66. Take the green rod in front of 2 uprights, but this time it goes behind BOTH the corner uprights. And now you can ignore it as we don't use it again—trim it back if it's a distraction, but not too short.

67. And now both the purple and pink uprights come down into the space between the corner uprights.

68. The orange rod goes in front of the first corner upright (blue) and behind the next corner upright (green).

69. The blue corner upright lies down beside it.

70. The yellow now passes in front of the green corner upright, behind the orange and out to the front. This yellow rod remains a lonely rod—don't bend down an upright to join it.

71. Now take the red rod—lying next to the blue—and...

72. ...lift it up to kink it.

73. Now lay it down again and weave in front of the green and orange and behind the yellow upright.

74. Lay the green corner rod down beside it.

75. Take the purple rod coming under the corner and lift to kink it.

76. Weave the purple rod in front of the orange and yellow and behind the red uprights.

77. Now you can see that by kinking these rods you have formed a pleasing blunt corner.

78. Lay the orange rod down beside the purple.

79. The blue rod goes in front of the yellow and red and behind the purple uprights, and out to the front, and the yellow lies down beside it.

80. The lonely yellow is now woven in front of the red and purple and behind the pink uprights.

81. And the red upright lies down beside it. You now have 4 pairs again, so can continue weaving as before, but as this is a short side you're already approaching a corner, so refer to steps 66 onwards and repeat.

82. Finish the border off as usual and trim. Remove handle liners.

83. Now go to **page 97** to add the handle.

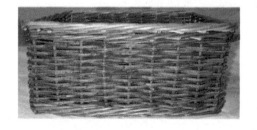

(SIMPLIFIED) FRAME BASKET

Dimensions: 30cm x 26cm

INGREDIENTS

6 x long 4ft/5ft buff rods, the butts of which should cover this circle.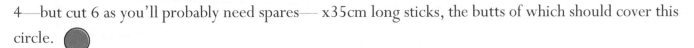

4—but cut 6 as you'll probably need spares— x35cm long sticks, the butts of which should cover this circle.

200gms 3ft Black Maul.

IMPORTANT Soak willow as advised on pages 4&5 and read page 6.

FRAME BASKET

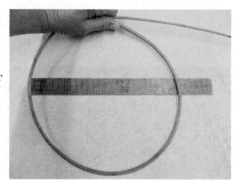

1. Take the longest, thickest rod and curve gently around your knee to discourage kinking. Now form a circle loosely with a diameter of no more than 25cm.

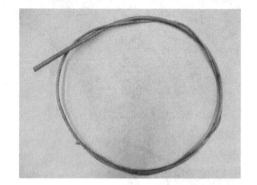

2. Wrap the thin end round the circle loosely, as shown. (O.K, it isn't a circle yet, but it soon will be!)

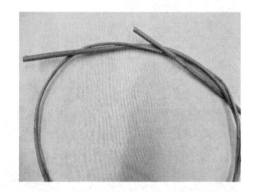

3. Insert the butt of a second rod into the circle space—not the circle itself—butt first, about 1/6 of the way round (going clockwise).

4. And wind round the circle loosely. You may find it easier to ease the 'loop' through rather than the tip—you'll see what I mean when you do it.

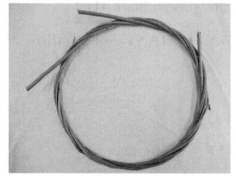

5. Take a third rod and repeat—just follow the groove, and you will see it all happens quite naturally.

6. Now add 3 more rods in the same way.

7. Trim the butts so that they lie against the circle.

Note: You must now complete steps 8 to 19 before the ring dries out—if you need a break, then wrap the ring. It is best in any case that all the work is completed before the ring dries out—dunk for a short while to prevent this.

8. Take 2 of the fattest sticks of same length and use the secateurs to point the sticks as shown. Ease round your knee very gently to form a curve.

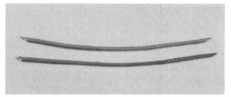

9. Insert the pointed end of one into the weave, and then do the same with the other end so that it's opposite.

10. Repeat with the other stick alongside the first, but with the butt at the opposite end.

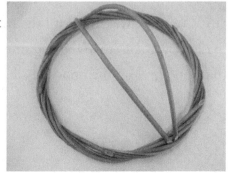

11. The next bit is a tad fiddly, and the sticks may pop out occasionally—just persevere! Don't worry about the other two ends: you can adjust them later when you weave them. Take a thin rod of brown willow and arrange like so, with the short tip end to the left and the rest of the rod coming under the ring towards you.

12. Now up and behind the right rib, in front of the left then under the circle and back to the front.

13. Take the rod behind the left rib, in front of the right, under the ring and back to the front.

14. Repeat stages 12 and 13.

15. Continue weaving until the rod runs out and then turn the basket over and leave the end on the inside. Now add another rod, butt end first on the opposite rib, and continue weaving as before.

16. At some point you will notice that the 'circle' is becoming oval—it's supposed to. Some of the butt ends might start to lift…

17. …so just trim them back.

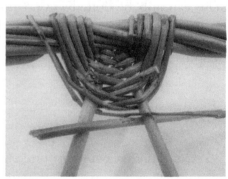

18. When it's time to insert a new butt, make sure it's always on the opposite rib.

19. Continue weaving as before, but now wrap around the ring twice every time.

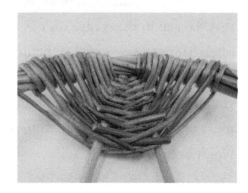

20. When you have completed approximately this much weaving, weave the opposite end in the same manner. If the ribs are troublesome before this, then start some of the weaving to hold them in place.

21. Slype two sticks on the back.

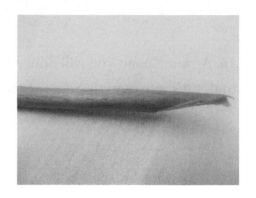

22. Insert one stick, slyped end down, into the weave. The next step is trial and (hopefully not) error.

 A few millimetres at a time, point the other end of the stick again and again and keep inserting it into the other end until it has the same curve as the middle two ribs.

This can only be done by eye—don't attempt to cut the second stick the same length as the first as they will probably be different lengths.

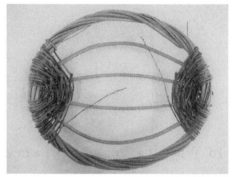

23. Continue weaving just one end only, always wrapping twice round the circle and starting each rod on opposite centre ribs, until the weave forms a straight line. Continue weaving but only wrap the circle once to maintain the straight line. When you get just beyond half way you'll need to start wrapping twice again, to meet the opposite end.

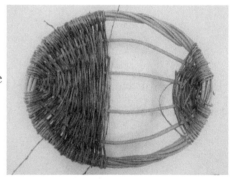

24. When you reach this point it gets a little more fiddly. You can see that the gap in the centre isn't as wide as the gap near the edge. This often happens as it's very difficult to judge the amount of wrap arounds needed to keep the gap equal. I used to work from each end equally and join in the middle, but that's the widest point and most on show, so it's better to tuck the join away at an end where it won't be so noticeable.

25. After weaving the gap a little more, the middle becomes too narrow, so insert a butt as usual, weave round the ring 2 or 3 times, and if that hasn't filled the space after working back to the middle, turn back and repeat.

26. Now insert the butt end of a rod like so.

27. Wrap the circle twice, return to the nearest rib, and then back to the circle again to fill the gap.

There is no exact method, and every basket will be different, but keeping an eye on the gap as you work will make the final join a lot easier.

28. Trim the ends—you will have to lift them slightly to do this. Try to cut on a slype so that the white ends face upwards in this pleasing pattern.

You can, of course, join in butts on any rib, but the end result is never so pleasing.

DRAGONFLY

INGREDIENTS

9 x Black Maul rods of similar length—can be GREEN.

1x shorter Black Maul rod—can be GREEN.

IMPORTANT: soak willow as advised on pages 4&5—unless using GREEN—and read page 6.

If you're puzzled by the lack of information in the list of ingredients it's because the rods can be as long as you like—3ft or 8ft! We make most of our dragonflies for events with 6ft plus, but you will find it easier with shorter rods to start with—leftovers from a basket project are ideal for this. Stick with Black Maul, as it's good and pliable. You can buy 'green' willow in the winter months only.

DRAGONFLY

1. Take the 5 longest rods and bunch them together. Now take the short rod and kink it a few centimetres up from the butt (fat end).

2. Wrap the short rod round itself and the bundle of rods.

3. Thread the tip end back through the weave—you may need your bodkin to help you to do this—and then pull tight.

4. Arrange the bundle of rods as shown—I'm using coloured rods to make the following process clearer.

5. Take the pink rod over the green and orange rods.

51

6. Take the orange rod over the pink and yellow rods.

7. Take the yellow rod over the orange and purple rods.

8. Take the purple rod over the yellow and green rods.

9. Take the green rod over the purple and pink rods.

10. Take the pink rod over the green and orange rods. Now continue with this weave until the rods run out, but first look at the next steps for shaping the weave.

11. To make the head wider, lay the weaver (yellow) as shown, away from the bound butts. Then weave as before.

12. When shaping the tail, you'll need to go narrow, so bring the weaver (yellow) close to the butts, and weave as before.

Tip: if a rod snaps, just re-insert it from where it snapped and carry on weaving.

13. When the rods have nearly run out, take one of them and wrap it twice round the others, as shown.

14. Now use your bodkin and push under the two rounds.

15. Thread the tip of the weaver through and pull tight.

16. You have completed the body.

17. For the wings take the remaining 4 rods and 'slype' (point) the butt ends as shown.

18. Ease a rod gently around your knee, following the curve of the rod. This will help the shaping of the wing. Insert the butt end of the rod through the head as shown.

19. Thread the tip end back through the head and then continue threading round the core until the wing is tight.

20. Repeat for the other side.

DRAGONFLY

21. Now do the same slightly further back.

22. Point a cane with secateurs and insert into the tummy of the dragonfly.

You have completed your first dragonfly—sit back and admire your handiwork.

(And then make some more.)

HEARTS

SIMPLIFIED HEART INGREDIENTS

These can be made from any size willow, but you'll find 4ft Black Maul about right to start with.

16 x 4ft Black Maul (brown or green), not too thick but 14 long and 2 short. (More if you like.)

IMPORTANT: soak willow as advised on pages 4&5—unless using GREEN— and read page 6.

1. Select 12 of the long rods—save the 2 longest—and then pull them around your knee, following the natural curve of the rod. Divide the bundle in two as shown, and then use an elastic band to hold the butt ends together, about 15 cm. up.

HEARTS

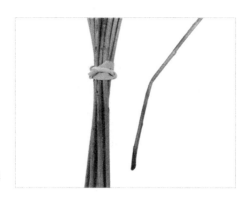

2. Take the shortest rod and kink it a few centimetres up from the butt end as shown.

3. Now hold the kinked rod against the bundle just below the elastic band and wrap it around itself and the bundle.

4. Continue wrapping and then use your bodkin to thread the tip of the willow back through the binding.

You can now remove the elastic band—cut it.

5. Now pull both sides of the willow down to form a heart shape and, using a short rod, bind and wrap as before.

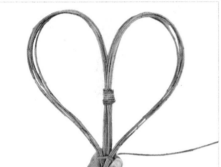

6. Ease the upper binding to achieve the heart shape you desire, and gently push down on the curves to get a wider heart.

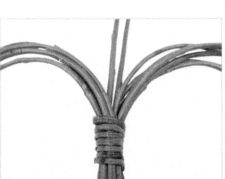

7. Slype (point with your secateurs) and insert the 2 long rods into the top binding—you may need your bodkin for this.

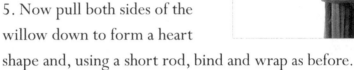

8. Wrap one rod round one side of the heart as shown, and then thread through the binding.

9. Now repeat for the other side. Your heart is complete. Trim the 'tail' if you want a more conventional heart shape.

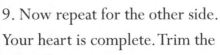

HEARTS (2)

1. When you've got the hang of them, why not include more rods? Or miss out the elastic band stage and upper binding all together—just hold the butts and then bend each set of rods over, hold them all in one hand, including the butt of a short rod, and wrap as before.

2. Insert the wrappers in the binding. (You'll need much longer, thinner rods for this method.)

3. Take the right hand rod and wrap around the trunk as shown.

4. Repeat with the left hand rod.

Now finish wrapping around each side and thread through the binding as before.

BUNTING

INGREDIENTS

As with so many of the fun projects in this book, what you use is rather up to you. The bunting pictured above is made from our own home grown willow when it is 'green', which is the best way to capture the colours.

For your first efforts I would suggest the following:

4ft Black Maul—longest rods and as many as you want to make. Green or brown.

Some cord—I used waxed cotton.

A block or something similar—for 4ft rods it will need to be about 11-12cm long.

IMPORTANT: soak willow as advised on pages 4&5—unless using GREEN—and read page 6.

BUNTING

1. Hold the block with it's end against the butt (fat) end of a rod and kink. (Obviously you'll use both hands.)

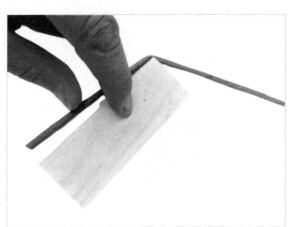

2. Move the block along and rest one end in the new corner and kink again.

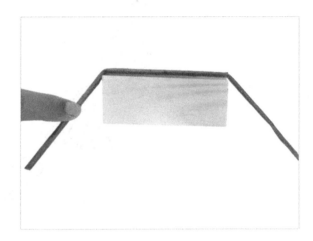

3. Repeat stage 2.

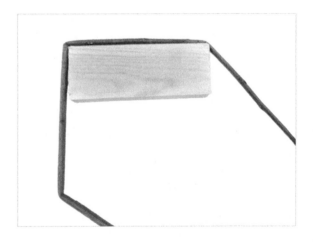

4. Hold the willow as shown with about a centimetre of the butt end showing, and a corner resting on the rod.

5. Now wind the willow round as shown.

6. Weave over and under…

7. …from side to side.

8. Now weave back, from side to side, but this time in and out of the weave you've already completed…

9. …over and under as before.

10. Thread the willow through the hole in the corner—you might need your bodkin to widen the hole.

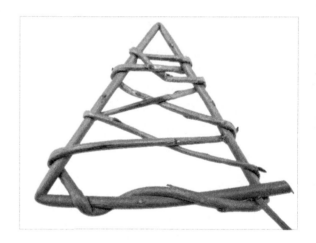

11. Thread the willow in and out and over the existing weaving at the start, and finish by threading through the hole in the other corner.

12. Trim ends and thread the cord through the holes in the corners to create the bunting.

CHRISTMAS

Willow has been used for centuries to celebrate Yuletide, so let me encourage you to embrace some traditional decorations this year.

The wreath has been part of our Christmas for many years, though nowadays it is rarely made of willow or other hedgerow material as it originally was. Go to **page 67** to make this very easy decoration and then display it proudly on your front door.

The kissing bough (bottom right) is a truly British Christmas decoration which is believed to date from the Middle Ages. It was certainly very popular in Tudor England, where it would be covered in greenery, nuts, berries and sweetmeats, with mistletoe hanging below, and an orange or apple suspended in the middle. Turn to **page 64** to construct one to hang in your own home.

The star has long been a part of Christmas, and I have no doubt that country children would have fashioned these for themselves. Go to **page 69** to make these to string across your room or hang from the tree.

As you know, the Christmas tree only appeared in this country in the Victorian era, but I have designed these little trees to go with the stars— **page 72** will show you how to make them.

Now take a weekend in early December, gather some greenery, cones and berries, and settle in for some real winter pleasure!

KISSING BOUGH

INGREDIENTS

10 x thick, long 4ft—or longer—Black Maul, brown or green. (Or use hedgerow material.)

Florists'/gardeners' wire.

Greenery such as trailing ivy, holly, rosehips, fir cones, mistletoe etc.

Apple/orange/small lantern (with battery candle) and narrow ribbon for hanging.

2.5m of wide ribbon and 2 tinsel sticks to make bows.

IMPORTANT: soak willow as advised on pages 4&5—unless using GREEN— and read page 6.

KISSING BOUGH

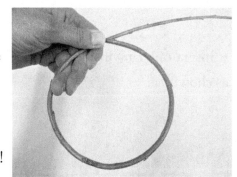

1. Take the longest, thickest rod and curve gently around your knee to discourage kinking. To encourage a tighter curve, hold the butt and rod tip in one hand, forming a circle, and then feed the tip through your other hand, holding it against the circle so that gradually the circle shrinks. You need to try this to see what I mean!

2. Now form a circle as large as you can while loosely winding the rod round itself. You can tuck the tip end back on itself to fasten, or use wire.

3. Insert a second rod, butt first, about 1/5 of the way round (going clockwise) and wind round the circle loosely, following the groove. To avoid kinking you may find it easier to ease the 'loop' through rather than the tip—you'll see what I mean when you do it.

4. Insert a 3rd rod and wind loosely in the same manner, following the groove.

5. Repeat with a 4th and 5th rod. Trim the ends so that they lie against the weave. Now make another ring roughly the same size.

6. Insert one ring inside the other and use the wire to fasten as shown.

7. Collect same trailing ivy, insert the end into the wire join, and then wind round, following the groove of one circle, and then the other. Repeat as many times as you like. If ivy is not available, then attach other evergreen with wire. In the early stages I like to wind some battery microlights round as well— the battery pack sits happily in the bottom, disguised by more greenery.

8. To make the bows, divide the broad ribbon into 4 equal pieces. Now arrange one piece as shown.

9. Cut a tinsel stick in half and wrap around the middle as you pinch the ribbon together. Repeat with the other pieces. Trim ends.

Now attach the bows and decorate how you wish, with holly, cones, mistletoe etc. Thread the thin ribbon through the top to suspend an apple, orange or lantern (with battery candle) in the centre.

WREATH

INGREDIENTS

20+ thick rods (brown or green) or hedgerow material.

(I've used 4ft Black Maul for the Christmas wreath instructions—see next page.)

Whatever you like for decoration—holly, ivy, cones, berries, fruit, nuts, ribbon, raffia etc. or leave it plain.

Florist/gardeners' wire.

IMPORTANT: soak willow as advised on pages 4&5—unless using GREEN—and read page 6.

WREATH

1. Repeat stages 1-5 of the kissing bough ring. (**page 65**). Trim.

2. Turn the circle over, butt side down, and insert a rod like so.

3. Weave clockwise as before, but this time you will notice that you are weaving against the groove. This is to achieve a fatter, lighter wreath than if you constantly follow the groove. Continue adding in rods, as many as you like, but evenly spaced. You can turn the wreath as many times as you like, depending on how fat you want it.

4. When you have finished, trim all the ends so they lie neatly on the back. Now turn the wreath over and decorate as you wish.

Why not make wreaths to celebrate other times of the year? Pictured left is one I made for Michaelmas— it's a lot of fun gathering the Autumn' harvest!

STARS

INGREDIENTS

As with all the fun projects, you can make these as large or as small as you wish. For the following instructions, you will need:

4ft Black Maul rods, brown or green.

A block or something similar—for 4ft rods it will need to be about 11-12cm long.

IMPORTANT: soak willow as advised on pages 4&5—unless using GREEN—and read page 6.

1. Hold the block against the butt end of the rod, about 1 cm in as shown, and kink it.

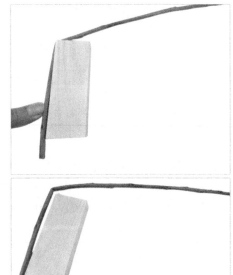

2. Now move the block along and kink again.

3. Repeat stage 2 twice more—you will now have 4 corners.

4. Hold the willow as shown.

5. Thread the willow under and over, easing the corner through the centre gap. You will, of course, be using both hands for this.

6. Under and over again.

7. Wrap the willow twice round the butt after adjusting the shape.

STARS

8. Now wrap once round an internal corner.

9. Continue wrapping each corner until you reach this stage.

10. Thread the willow through the gap as shown.

11. Wind the willow in and out of this gap to tie it off.

Now trim, and either thread on to waxed cord or hang individually.

WANDS

You will need a 5ft rod for this.

1. With the 11/12cm block, kink the rod about 30cm in from the butt.

2. Repeat 3 more times.

Now form the star—page 69, step 2 onwards.

I have used Vitellina—a variety we grow— to make this wand. However, we generally make them out of 6ft rods, and use a 15cm block.

Try to use thick, 'stumpy' rods so that the handle is a good thickness.

CHRISTMAS TREES

INGREDIENTS

As with all the fun projects, you can make these as large or as small as you wish. For the following instructions you will need:

Long and thin/medium 4ft Black Maul rods, brown or green.

Cord to thread them with.

A block or something similar—for 4ft rods it will need to be about 8-10cm long.

IMPORTANT: soak willow as advised on pages 4&5—unless using GREEN—and read page 6.

CHRISTMAS TREES

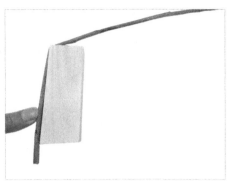

1. Hold the block against, and about 1cm from, the butt (fat) end of a rod and kink.

2. Move the block along and rest one end in the new corner and kink again.

3. Repeat stage 2 until you have 4 corners.

4. Now arrange as shown, holding the butt to the right. (Don't cut the willow—this photo is cropped!)

5. Wrap around the 'trunk'…

6. …and then as shown…

7. …weaving from side to side, in and out, but treating the centre column as one.

8. …until you reach the top.

9. At this point you can make a little hanging loop if you wish and thread to the back.

10. Thread the willow from side to side, in and out of the weave, back to the trunk, and wind in and out of the gap here to fasten off. (You may need your bodkin to help with this.) Trim.

GETTING STARTED—THE BASE

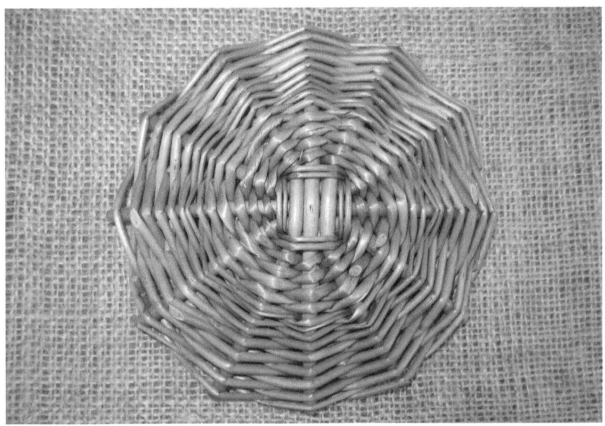

    All of the 'round' baskets in this book begin with this base. Take your time with this as it will determine the shape of the basket and how it 'sits' on its rim. First select which basket you'd like to make from those in this book and cut 6 base sticks accordingly.

1. Take one of the 6 base sticks and, using a bodkin, bradawl or sharp knife, pierce the middle of it and then 2 more.

2. Thread the other three through the holes in these three, being sure to alternate thin and fat ends, which will make for a more even basket.

PAIRING

(This is the weave you're about to do.)

3. Now take 2 of the longest, thinnest buff weavers and insert the tips—the thin ends—in through the gap beside three sticks. I've used coloured rods to make the process clearer.

4. Take the pink rod over 3 sticks and the purple rod under.

5. Take the purple rod over the pink rod and 3 sticks and the pink rod under 3 sticks.

6. Take the pink rod over the purple rod and 3 sticks, and take the purple under. (You can 'trap' the tip ends at this point.)

7. Now you're back to the beginning again.

NOTE: You'll naturally be turning the work as you weave but I've photographed it in the same position to make things clearer.

8. Repeat the process: purple over pink and 3 rods etc., until you've been round twice. Pull the rods towards you as you work.

Tip: Take two lengths of string and twist them together; this is the weave you're doing, only you're capturing a stick with each twist. Don't worry if the rods split at the beginning—you're going round tight corners.

9. Now we need to divide the sticks, so take the lower rod over the upper rod, and the upper rod under ONE stick, as shown, pulling the rods towards you and into the middle to avoid gaps.

10. Now the upper rod goes under the next stick and back towards you.

11. Same again.

12. And again! Continue dividing the sticks as you pair round them, pulling the RODS towards you, but pushing the STICKS away to create a slightly domed shape, and turning the base as you work. Try to keep the spokes of the wheel the same distance apart and weave tightly, but not so tightly that you distort a base stick.

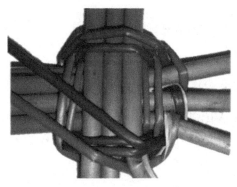

13. When the rods 'run out', you have to join in two more. Do this at the same time: if one rod is longer than the other, trim as shown, each rod coming out of its own gap and resting on a stick.

14. Insert 2 new rods, butt (fat end) first into the gaps beside and to the right of the finished rods.

15. Weave the new green rod precisely as before.

16. Weave the orange rod, as before. Continue pairing until these rods run out, and then join in as already described, but this time TIP first. As you weave make sure you pull the rods towards you and concentrate on creating a slightly domed shape, though it is better to have an exaggerated dome than no dome at all. Weave in more rods, as necessary. End on tips and tuck these into the weave.

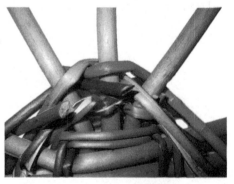

17. Trim the rods.

Now trim the sticks.

You have finished the base.

With larger bases try starting 2 pairs opposite each other after the initial 4 rods are woven—it will make the base more even.

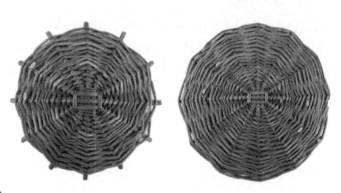

STAKING UP

You will need 24 uprights, the size/thickness according to the project you've chosen.

Now, depending on the basket you're making, you need to do one of the following:

For all 'upright' baskets—the apple, waste and log, for example—you must 'slype' the butt end of the rod on the **'belly'**: that is, use your secateurs or knife to make a point on the butt on the side where the rod curves inwards.

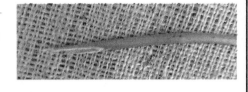

And generally for all other baskets that you want to flow outwards or be slightly rounded, it is better to 'slype' on the **'back'**: that is, use your secateurs or knife to make a point on the butt on the side where the rod curves outwards.

1. Insert your bodkin and then the slyped rods either side of each stick as far they will go, so that the slyped edge faces down and the dome of the base is pointing up. Wet the base and rod butts first to make this easier, or dip the butts in petroleum jelly or similar. Use your (greased if you like) bodkin to widen the gap.

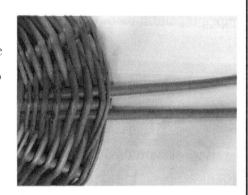

2. Now would be a good time to put a weight on the base to hold it steady.

Using a bodkin or knife, prick each rod just out from the base and lift and lower.

3. Lift all the rods and tie them at the top: elastic is ideal for this as it grips. There are other methods but this is best for beginners. Make sure the tie isn't lopsided and that the uprights aren't leaning in. Gather opposites to prevent bunching. Tie as high as you can as this will make the shaping of the basket much easier. Now, depending on the shape of your basket, arrange the rods by easing them out or in, until they mirror the actual basket you plan on making.

THE UPSETT

'Upsetting' is the weave that we do first to hold the uprights in position. For the purposes of this book—and most stake and strand baskets—we shall begin with a '**3 rod wale**'.

3 ROD WALE

1. Select 6 long, thin, buff weavers of similar length.

Arrange 3 of the rods—tips first—as shown.

2. Take the left hand rod (green) in front of two uprights, over the top of two rods, behind the next upright, and then out to the front.

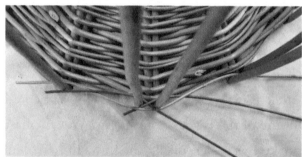

3. Repeat with the rod that is now furthest to the left (pink).

4. And again with the rod that is now furthest to the left (blue).

Continue with this weave.

5. When the rods run out, trim so that you have 3 butts coming from 3 consecutive spaces.

6. Insert the butt end of 3 weavers under, and to the right of, the 3 butt ends.

7. Take the rod furthest to the left (yellow) in front of 2 uprights, behind one, and out to the front.

8. Take the rod furthest to the left (purple) in front of 2 uprights, behind one, and out to the front.

9. Take the rod furthest to the left (orange) in front of 2 uprights, behind one, and out to the front.

Now keep weaving (waling) until these rods run out, paying especial attention to controlling the uprights, keeping them vertical, if slyped on the belly, and curving out slightly, if slyped on the back.

When these rods run out, cut tips so they appear in consecutive spaces as before. Consider repeating with another 6 rods to further establish the shape.

10. Now very <u>gently</u> 'rap' the weaving down. Use a ruler to measure the height of the weaving. Don't make the mistake of rapping harder to even the height—it can distort the sides and even make them bulge. Far better to ease the weaving up with your finger tips to make it even.

You have finished the waling.

ALTERNATIVE UPSETT

Once you have completed one basket you might like to try a more professional way to wale from the base. This will help cover the join between the base and the uprights. In all essentials it is exactly the same as a normal wale, but first remove the weight from the base and lay the work on its side, with the bottom of the base facing you. You will need 12 rods.

1. Lift all the rods and tie them at the top: elastic is ideal for this as it grips. Don't worry about the shape at this stage. Now with the bottom of the base facing you, use your bodkin to ease the left-hand upright away from the base stick. This will really help with spacing the uprights when weaving.

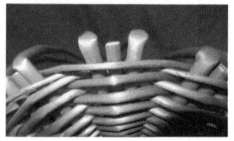

2. Insert 3 tips to the left of an upright as shown.

3. Take the right-hand rod behind and then between the first upright and the base stick. Ease the left-hand upright to the left.

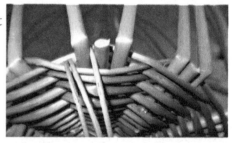

4. Take the second rod in front of the first upright and then behind the next.

5. Take the third rod in front of 2 uprights and then behind and between the next upright and base stick. Now we start the wale proper, in front of 2 uprights and behind the next, always easing the uprights apart and wedging the rod between the upright and the base stick where appropriate.

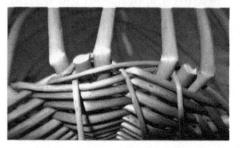

6. When you are half way round start 3 more rods as before and weave with these, dropping them when you catch up with the original three and so on.

7. The work needs to be upright before joining in the butts. Do this when all the base stick ends are covered. Adjust the tie up or down to encourage the shaping of the basket.

8. A tip when weaving is to pull each rod sharply to the right and pushing it in with your thumb.

9. It should help with preventing kinks in the weave and encourage a smooth flow.

10. Finish the wale. Rap down as usual.

11. For a wale further up the basket, join in 3 rods as shown on **page 80** but also join in 3 rods opposite and wale as already described.

SIDING

'Siding' simply refers to the weave used on the side of a basket. For the purposes of this book I shall be using the following: **Slewing** and **French Randing**. There are many more types of weave, and you have already used two: **Pairing** and **3 Rod Wale**. However, this is a book for beginners and we'll keep it simple.

SLEWING

This is a very useful weave as it builds up quickly, and is easy to do.

1. Insert the BUTT end of a weaver into a space and weave in and out 3 or 4 times.

2. Now lay another rod (butt end) on top of the first and weave with the pair as if they were one rod.

3. When you reach halfway round stop weaving. Now insert the butt of a new rod into the next gap and weave in and out 3 or 4 times.

4. And then add another rod and weave as a pair.

5. When you catch up with the original pair, drop these and continue weaving with the originals.

6. As each lower rod of the pair 'runs out', insert the butt of a new rod on top.

7. Continue weaving with the top pair. If both rods are of similar length, then drop the bottom one early and insert a new one on top.

Play this game of 'chase', joining in as before. Shape the sides of the basket as you work. Remove the elastic when you have slewed a few centimetres and feel that the uprights are controlled enough.

Rap down very gently every 5-10cm, and ease the weaving up as necessary, making sure the height is even all the way round.

3 Rod Slew

Once you are used to slewing with 2 rods, you can see how easy it would be to slew with 3 or even more rods. There are no hard and fast rules, but I would tend to introduce more rods in consecutive spaces, and do the same when joining in. Multiple rod slewing is ideal when you only have very thin weavers. However, never change from 2 rod to 3 or more in one basket as it will look a little odd, unless you put a break between them with another weave such as a wale.

FRENCH RANDING

This next weave isn't as good as controlling the uprights as the other 3 weaves already mentioned, so I would only use it when you are happy with the shape of your basket. If you want to use just this weave for the siding, then maybe do 2 lots of waling first to establish and control the shape.

1. Sort 24 weavers of roughly the same length and thickness, preferably only slightly thinner than the upright at this stage. Now insert the butt of one rod into a gap and weave in front of the next upright to the right, behind the next and out to the front.

2. Insert another rod to the left of the first and weave in the same manner.

3. And insert another rod to the left and weave as before.

4. Continue inserting the remaining rods until you have just 2 left to do.

5. Insert the butt end of a remaining rod (pink) into the gap under the last rod…

6. …and weave as before, keeping under the last rod, but over the first part of the weaving.

7. Insert the final rod (purple) under the weaving and to the left of the pink rod, and weave as before, keeping the purple rod under the pink but above the first weaving.

8. You should now have one rod protruding from every space.

9. Take any rod (purple in this case) and weave it in front of one upright, behind the next and out to the front.

10. Take the next rod to the left—in this case pink—and weave it in front of one upright, behind the next and out to the front.

11. And again. Now continue with each rod in turn until you arrive at the beginning where you will notice that there are two pairs of rods coming from each gap.

12. Take the lower rod of the purple pair and weave as shown—as you did before.

13. Take the lower rod of the pink pair and weave as before, keeping underneath the purple.

You now have 24 rods coming from each gap. Now repeat this 'circuit' again and again, concentrating on the shape, until the weavers run out.

Rap down gently and/or ease the weaving up to get an even height.

You can achieve various interesting effects using layers of French Randing:

checks (see back cover and page 18), spirals (start 12 of each colour opposite each other) and stripes (see page 18, but the second layer sits on top).

BORDERS

The border is the final stage of any basket, unless you're adding handles, lids etc., and there are dozens to choose from.

For the purposes of this book I am just demonstrating three: the **3 rod border** and the **5 rod behind 1**, and the **4 rod behind 2 for square work** (see page 39). The first is pretty straight forward, but the second gives a much better finish, and is more forgiving if the uprights are too close together. Start with the 3 rod border and when you're confident move on to the 5 rod behind 1.

3 ROD BORDER

This is one of the simplest, though not as simple as a 'trac' border, which I am not showing as it looks dreadful if the basket isn't perfectly round!

1. Using an implement that measures approximately 1cm high, lay it to the right of every rod and bend the rod over it and then stand it up again.

2. Take any upright and bend it down behind the one to the right.

3. Repeat with the next upright to the right (orange).

4. And again with the next upright to the right (purple).

You now have 3 uprights lying down.

5. Take the rod furthest to the left (green) in front of one upright—it's two really, but the purple is lying down— and behind the next and out to the front.

6. Now take the upright furthest to the left (yellow) and lay it down beside this rod.

7. Take the rod furthest to the left (orange) in front of one upright, behind the next, and out to the front.

8. Take the upright furthest to the left (red) and lay it down beside this rod.

9. Repeat these two actions with the final rod (purple) and upright (blue), and you will have 3 pairs of rods in consecutive spaces.

TIP: If a rod snaps, don't worry—just trim and insert it beside the broken end. If an upright snaps, just trim back to waling and stick the remainder of the rod in beside the stump.

10. Take the right-hand rod (yellow) of the left-hand pair over the two other pairs, in front of an upright, behind the next, and out to the front.

11. Lay the upright furthest to the left (green) down beside it.

12. Take the right-hand rod (red) of the left-hand pair over the two other pairs, in front of an upright, behind the next, and out to the front.

13. Lay the upright furthest to the left (orange) down beside it. Now continue this process all the way round.

14. When you arrive back at the beginning you will see that there is just one upright remaining and 3 pairs of rods lying down.

15. Take the right-hand rod (purple) of the left-hand pair in front of the upright and then behind to thread back to the front. (You may need your 'bodkin' for this.) To avoid kinking, try taking the rod in a wide loop before threading through. (See page 96, 17a.)

16. Now thread the upright (blue) through to lay down beside it.

17. Take the right-hand rod (yellow) of the left-hand pair over the other two pairs, then thread to the inside and back out again.

18. Take the right-hand rod (red) of the left-hand pair over the last remaining pair and the next rod, then thread through to the inside below the bent upright, and then out under all the weave.

19. Take the right-hand rod (blue) of the last pair over the next two rods, then thread through to the inside under the bent upright and back to the front under all the weave. The border is now complete and it only remains to trim all the rods so that they lie against an upright.

5 ROD BEHIND 1

Once you have mastered the 3 rod border you will find this quite straightforward.

1. Using an implement that measures approximately 1cm high, lay it to the right of every rod and bend the rod over it and then stand it up again. You are now ready to start the border.

2. Bend any upright down and behind the one to the right.

3. Repeat with the next upright to the right.

4. And so on until you have 5 uprights lying down as shown.

5. Take the rod furthest to the left in front of one upright—it's actually four, but three are lying down— behind the next, and out to the front.

6. Lay the upright furthest to the left down beside it.

7. Take the rod furthest to the left in front of one upright, behind the next, and out to the front.

8. Lay the upright furthest to the left down beside it. Repeat with the other 3 rods.

9. You now have 5 pairs of rods.

10. Take the right-hand rod of the left-hand pair in front of one upright, behind the next, and out to the front.

11. Lay the upright furthest to the left down beside it. Continue in this way, taking the right hand rod, and then laying the upright down…

12. …until you arrive back at the beginning again.

13. Take the right-hand rod of the left-hand pair in front of the upright. The trick now is to thread it behind the bent upright and out to the front; I either deliberately kink it at the point it passes behind to make it easier, or make a big loop. (See 17a.)

14. Thread the upright in beside it—I usually make a big loop first to stop it kinking. (See 17a.)

15. Now take the right-hand rod of the left-hand pair in where the last pair come out, and then out to the front.

16. Take the right-hand rod of the left-hand pair in where this last rod came out, but over all the border except for the top bit; that is, you go in under one rod. Now come out under all the border rods. (See 17b.) Repeat with the last 3 pairs.

17. You will now have one rod coming from every gap. Trim all rods back to an upright, inside and out.

(a) Making a big loop to prevent kinking.

(b) Going under ONE rod of the border but coming out under ALL the border. (Red highlight.)

When you're a bit more experienced, why not try 5 rod behind 2? (Lay 5 rods down behind 2 uprights and weave as before.) Or 4 behind 1 or 2?

HANDLES

The following instructions are for two types of handles: shopper and log.

SHOPPER

1. Ease the handle gently round your knee, following its natural curve, and then slype either end on the inner curve as shown.

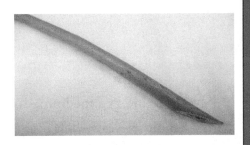

2. Insert the fat end of the handle one side as far as it will go—wetting or greasing will help with this—and then gently ease it over to the other side and insert it there in the same way. Trim the thinner end of the handle until you get the required height.

3. Cut 2 pieces of waste buff about 3cm long and slype to form pegs.

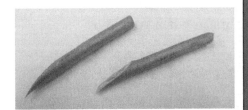

4. Using your bodkin, make a hole through the handle between the waling.

5. Insert one of the pegs.

6. Hammer it through and then trim off the excess. Repeat other side.

7. Slype and insert a medium 4ft/5ft buff rod to the left of one end of the handle as shown, as far as it will go.

8. Carefully wrap the handle with the rod 3 times, bringing it back to the inside. To avoid kinking you may find it easier to push the 'loop' through rather than the tip as you wrap—you'll see what I mean when you do it.

9. Thread the tip of the rod through the waling—and to the left of—the handle, and then to the outside. Use your bodkin for this.

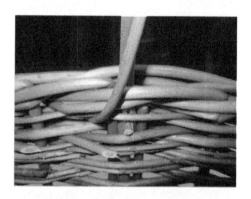

10. Insert another rod to the right of the first...

11. ...and wrap as before, following the path of the first rod.

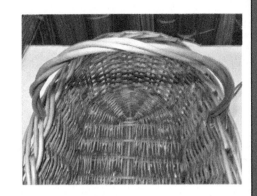

12. Insert a third rod to the right of the second...

13. ...and wrap as before. Repeat with one more rod.

14. Do the same with the other side of the handle, following the existing wrapping. If there are any gaps remaining, insert another rod one side to fill it, but only if the gap is wide enough.

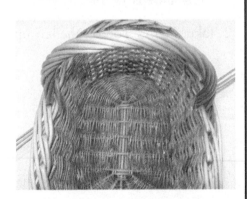

15. Take the remainder of the rods on the outside up and to the left.

16. Wrap around the handle and down to the left.

17. Using your bodkin, thread through the waling to the inside and lose the ends by threading in and out of the waling. Repeat on the other side. Now trim.

ALTERNATIVE METHOD

There are many ways to finish the handle wrapping, but below is one of the prettiest.

1. Repeat steps 1– 14 .

2. Take the first rod on the left up to the left…

3. …round the handle and back to the front to form a cross.

4. Thread to the inside.

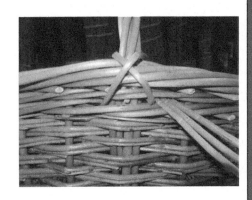

5. Repeat with the second rod.

6. And the third and fourth. Lose the tips in the waling.

TIP

As I have already said, when adding the rods to wrap the handle there may be a gap which you can fill with another rod. Depending on the thickness of the wrappers, you can usually manage 4 aside. However, the temptation is to squeeze in another rod when there is inadequate space. In this instance it is better to leave the gap and space the wrappers as best you can—if you try to force another in it can cause a bulge.

HANDLES FOR LOG BASKETS

1. Slype and insert 2 rods beside an 'upright', 3,4 or 5 'uprights' apart. The size of the gap should allow ample space for an adult hand.

2. Take the right hand rod through the waling to the left of the other rod and pull through until the handle measures 6– 8cm high, depending on the size of the basket, and then kink the rod on the inside by pulling it upright and then leave it.

3. You are now going to 'rope' the other rod. Simply grasp the rod near the tip with both hands as shown.

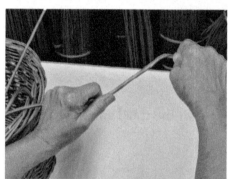

4. Move your right hand in a 'cranking' action while you feed the rod through the left, moving your hand down slowly until you've roped the whole rod.

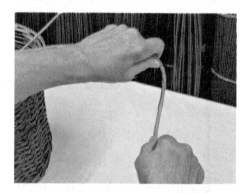

5. The rod will look like this when you've finished.

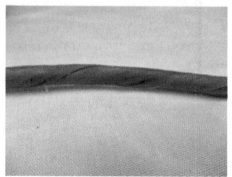

6. Wind the roped rod—you will have to keep it twisted—round the handle as shown, and bring it to the outside.

7. Thread through to the inside to the right of the handle using your bodkin.

8. Bring the twisted rod to the outside again.

9. Now wrap round the handle again as shown.

10. Thread the rod through to the left of the handle.

11. Bring the remainder to the front and wrap the handle as before.

12. Rope the rest of the handle that you left on the inside, bring to the front and wrap.

13. Thread to the inside, bring back to the outside, and then wrap again.

14. Thread all the remaining ends in and out of the waling to make the handle secure.

15. Repeat for the other handle.

RECOMMENDED READING

There are a lot of basket making books out there, and most will offer something new and interesting. Here are three that I can thoroughly recommend:

The Complete Book of Basketry Techniques *Sue Gabriel and Sally Goymer*

Publisher: David & Charles plc

ISBN 0-7153-0934-X and 978-0715309346

Basket Borders *The Basketmakers' Association*

Publisher: The Basketmakers' Association

ISBN 0-9525541-3-5

Willow Work *Mary Butcher*

Publisher: Mary Butcher, Canterbury 1995

ISBN 0-952554100 and 978-0952554103

NOTE FROM THE AUTHOR

If you have found this book helpful it would be much appreciated if you could leave a review/rating on Amazon or Goodreads.

Thank you!

Made in the USA
Las Vegas, NV
10 February 2024